Messengers from the Sky

written by Albert Karp

illustrated by Stephen Snider

**McGraw-Hill
School Division**

New York   Farmington

Five thousand years ago, when the King of Egypt had an important announcement to make he didn't send e-mail. He didn't send a fax, make a phone call, or appear on TV or radio. None of these were things invented yet.

What did the king do? He sent out a group of pigeons. Not just any pigeons. Pigeons that can find their way home even if they are many miles away. These special birds are called homing pigeons.

Over 2,000 years ago, homing pigeons carried news about who won the Olympic Games to all the cities in Greece.

Some years later, in Rome, judges would take homing pigeons with them to work early in the morning. The birds would fly back to their homes carrying messages to the judges' families.

Because they carried messages, people gave homing pigeons another name—carrier pigeons.

How do carrier pigeons find their way back home? No one is really sure.

Some people think that pigeons are born knowing how to use the position of the Sun to lead them. Some people think the pigeons use tiny magnets inside their bodies to find their way home. Some people think that they use their sense of smell.

And some people think that pigeons do all of these things.

GERMANY

There are many ways homing pigeons have helped people.

In the 1800s a man named Baron de Reuter used them to bring the news to people in Germany, France, and Belgium.

When airplanes were a new invention, sometimes pigeons were taken along. Then, if the plane crashed, the birds could fly back for help.

Pigeons were used by armies all over the world. They carried secret messages about an enemy's location. Pigeons also brought messages that asked for more soldiers, or for more food and guns.

The most amazing stories about homing pigeons tell how they helped our country during times of war. In 1917 the United States was fighting a war in Europe. Here are the stories of three homing pigeons that helped the U.S. Army.

One pigeon was called "Big Tom." One afternoon he was sent with an important message taped to his leg. Lots of bullets and noisy bombs were going off in the air all around him.

But "Big Tom" flew 24 miles in 25 minutes (almost a mile a minute) and delivered the message to exactly the right place. This was even more amazing because he had been shot in the leg and in the chest.

Another pigeon hero of the First World
War was "The Mocker." He was shot in
the eye while he was flying with his
message. But still he finished his journey.
He delivered news that told where the
enemy kept their big guns. In this way,
"The Mocker" helped to save many lives.

"President Wilson" was a homing pigeon named for the man who was President of the United States during the war. "President Wilson" rushed through heavy fog and gunfire to deliver a message about some soldiers who were in terrible danger. He made it, even though he was shot in the leg.

Homing pigeons are not used to deliver messages in war any more.

Today the pigeons are raced against each other. Pigeons are taken from their homes, or lofts, to a place 60, 100, or even 400 miles away. Then they are let loose.

The owners keep a record of how long it takes for each pigeon to come back. The fastest one to arrive is the winner of the race.

This story about pigeons is hard to believe. But it's true. Once a man from New York sent a friend in South America his best homing pigeon. Once it got there, the pigeon decided to fly home to New York.

The pigeon flew over land. It crossed the ocean. It kept flying in all kinds of weather for more than two thousand miles. The trip took three months but it was a success. The homing pigeon made it home.